Early in the Morning

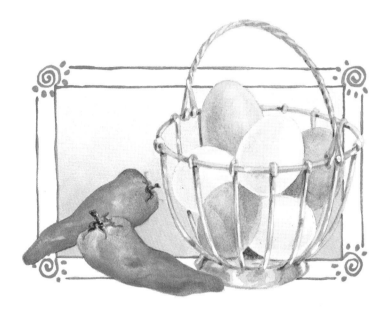

Lada Kratky

Illustrated by DJ Simison

HAMPTON-BROWN BOOKS
MANY CULTURES, MANY LANGUAGES...MANY POSSIBILITIES!™

Good morning!
What do you want to eat?

I want
some custard, Mom.

No. You can't have custard
so early in the morning.

4

Then I want
some cake, Mom.

No. You can't have cake
so early in the morning.

Then I want
some pizza, Mom.

Okay. Here's a pizza
with bacon and eggs on top!